Alison Fell is a Scottish poet and novelist. Her first volume
of poems, *Kisses for Mayakovsky*, won the Alice Hunt Bartlett
Award (National Poetry Society) in 1984. Her stories, poems
and essays are widely anthologised and she edited and
contributed to the experimental prose-fiction collections,
The Seven Deadly Sins, *The Seven Cardinal Virtues*, and
Serious Hysterics, all published by Serpent's Tail. Her five
novels include *Mer de Glace*, winner of the Boardman Tasker
Award (1991), and *The Pillow Boy of the Lady Onogoro* (1994),
which has been widely translated. Her work was featured in
the BBC Scotland TV film *Whispers in the Dark*, in winter
1995–96. Alison Fell lives in London.

D1420063

Dreams, *like* heretics

new and selected poems

ALISON FELL

Library of Congress Catalog Card Number: 97-067084

A catalogue record for this book is available from
the British Library on request

First published in 1997 by Serpent's Tail, 4 Blackstock
Mews, London N4; and 180 Varick Street, 10th floor,
New York, NY 10014
Website: www.serpentstail.com

Set in 9pt Stone Serif by Avon Dataset Limited, Bidford on Avon,
Warwickshire
Printed in Great Britain by Mackays of Chatham PLC, Chatham, Kent

For my hill and valley friends,
and of course for Ivan

Contents

from Kisses for Mayakovsky

from The Crystal Owl

In memoriam D.C.,
Poems 1993–95

Stalker

If I say your leaving
puts years on me,
it's because I know too well
how winter creaks in
on rickety ankles
to cull the loveless

It frightens me
when you go away in the vast
aeroplane that is my mother's
body. In these prairie

moments I pummel you, laughing
and crying, for nothing
will stop you now

Love travels the map
with her tomahawk. Love
secretes herself,
arthritic, in the green
nodding sea of the tundra

I want you against me
like a big cat,
I want you to surround me
like Red Indians surround
covered wagons, with their

war-whoops and grease-paint
and pheasant feathers

coming at me for the kill
in the high black movie night
with its white scent
of smoke and stars

Nothing so simple

Through the window the low sun,
insistent, reflects on the posters:
Fleurs des Pyrénées, with the red
whorled poppies that tear at me,
and suddenly

I'm with you
on that flaring ride past sand-
bergs or through the dappled
smoky threat of the *souk.*

Under the friction of our feet
freedom unwraps itself superbly
and we believe ourselves
substantial, are so, far
from the fear-clouds, obedience,
and the grinding wheels of the rain.

Nothing so simple
as thinking this, as being there,
throats thick with heat and distance,
two hot coals of us
in the tongs of the sun.

Hotel Salammbô

On the Avenue Bourghiba a low
jet over the feather-palms
precedes lightning. People flee
like birds in the black
rain. Tomorrow she'll be

leaving, but in the meantime
give coins to the beggarwoman,
thanks for the fallen dates
they flatten underfoot, these
prodigal smears. On the bed,

the sheets are frayed.
Gurgle of the shower. Now
he's on the green crumbling
balcony, now brown behind her
in the wardrobe mirror, noble,
tall as a camel. She combs

her hair out and up, thinking
of sand-winds, and how the Sahara
would be a hard sea to cross.
Already his right eye's turning
towards matters that concern him;

only the left one, salt-fringed,
is petrified with loss.
Trams rumble on the Rue de Grèce.
She closes the shutters, sinks
in the listening room. Now

she is sand itself and scattered;
beneath, luck like a mosaic shows
the buried glitter of its pattern.

In his hand there's a ferry-ticket.
Tanith with her geometric arms
will hoist her crescent moon
above the tide.

Adana airport, 09.00 hours, February 14

The sun bites
in, bleaches: no
telling where the silence

begins, and the relentless
shimmer – on the snow-ridge
of the skyline

or here on the flat
tarmac stretched
like a tambourine-skin

They are sliding you into
a small plane sleek
as a swordfish

The terminal is a glass shack
punched by the winds
of Syria, where tourists

watch, incurious, from
their queue of suitcases.
The runway ends at eternity.

Out here
we are under guard: grey
uniforms, guns. I have forgotten
the Turkish for husband.

Pain stores up in me
like static. All metal, like time,
has become lethal,

a modern grid of accident,
forms in triplicate, death
by bureaucracy.

There is a myth here they refuse
to read –

this ambulance, darling, this
mad dash a whisky-promise
I never expected to keep

– simply the female is foreign
and hysterical.

The next scene's pure
slapstick: a passport snatch,
a startled fusillade

of radios. They charge
across the apron, a herd
of extras, flattening

their holsters down
against their thighs
like bouncing breasts

The rest
is a vanishing act:
a morning jet-trail

fading across blue,
wafer of a white moon. The quiet
engine of your breath.

O my heart we're so smooth
and aloof here,
we could tongue the terrible

ear of the Gods.
I tell you they're all
Turks, all of them, trained to

smile honey and comfort
and save weak women
from the bitter truth.

In the fuselage you lie
shaven, tucked up,
terminal in tubes –

my hope, our plane, this cramped
Valentine, miraculous
hands of the pilots

At fifty thousand feet I clutch
your big toe like a talisman
and won't let go

Pieta 2

death has scooped you
out of me
broken the cradle
of your arms
exiled you to the abominable
mantelpiece of candlesticks

I have a high room
filled with fury
where the fridge
ticks endlessly

neighbours rattle at the door
like dry beans
I take nothing from anyone

when I shut my eyes
I am totally invisible

only death can see me
tangled like a black goat
in the thicket of sheets

if I cannot have you
no one else will do

I will drool like an idiot
eat figs and ashes

stuff death
into my mouth
and suck it like a thumb

Angel/Gargoyle

One of us, darling,
is disembodied:
the other hoists lime-
stone wings above the graveyard
and clings and clings

I live by compression:
already I bear the weight
of two – not just
my own frank flesh
but the death
I gave birth to

Didn't I think
I had seen grace,
didn't I let you go
with the stargazers,

in the name of freedom
loosed you to the high
incommensurable light?

All spirit now, you ice
the air eternally
with your white ash,

while I am a crude
joke of heaven – snout,
claws, granite belly
scaled like an armadillo

Do you circle me,
aimless, inaudible, concealing
your frequency?

I live in the noise
of idiot anthems,
in the dark below the self
where the faithful
cross their fingers

Who has stopped dead
and who gone forward,
now time neither shines
nor flows between us?

Dreams brief as photos
keep their counsel,
go to the fire like heretics,
holding their tongues,

and nothing answers
me: the bright clouds
write no letters, leave
no talismans between my thighs

Listen to me darling: last night
on my grotesque pillow
I made love to you
like a gargoyle, like an angel

Heroides

Any woman would have
turned you into Ulysses:
this was your journey
and your intent

How it shone in your eyes
and how we loved you
for it,
those of us left on the shore
pretending to scorn
your swaggering step,
hands empty, hair
wild as bees' nests
in the scattering wind

We have all cried out
to you from Carthage,
from Troy and Aulis,
yet not one of us cared
about spoils

It was your need alone
to bring them to us,
to return triumphant

You thought we wanted
goatskins, camphor, gifts
of white silk from Damascus,
when all we yearned for
was a footstep on the thresh-
hold, the delirious proof
of eyes

But you had to vanish
into the storm,
feel the rain
chew at your face
and the wind beat the mast
bent as an olive tree

You would go
seeking whirlpools,
dolphins, ports
where the houses
hang white as gulls
above the sea

Light fell from you
and frittered itself
on the waters
while we scuttled
in the shallows like crabs:
we tried
to hang on

Letters flew to us
from Alexandria,
from the Cap Affrique

If we hardly slept a wink
we knew this was
what you wanted –

How you needed
to be longed for, to be
glimpsed in the distance
like a white sail
and held in our hearts

In the solitary night
you turned us
like a key in your hand

All this we assented to
but could not save you

For we were not custodians
of the cruel blueprint
fate had traced

You should have come
majestic up the estuary,
dwarfing the pilots
and the tugs

You should have come
like a bright ferry full
of songs and dancing

All the horseshoes
we hammered into the decks
for luck!
All the charms
and amulets we hung
from the arms of the warrior!

Still your treasure-ship
came back empty,
the hull holed
and the proud masts broken

On the whiteness of our bones
we wrote your name
We offered up everything
We were stronger than sorrow

If only you would live!

Love is our cargo now,
delicate and durable
In our bodies
we preserve you
like a wildflower pressed
between the leaves of a book

When tears open us
over and over again
we will discover you
not in great deeds
but all fragile and fine
in the foaming pages

Pieta 1

Behind us, eucalyptus
on the wind, the unmistakable
scent of Anatolia

You the mourning which weights
the bag of my beak

I the pelican born
of necessity, clumsy as an airship
lumbering for takeoff,
hardly clearing the beach

Who in the crowded ports
will receive us, when sadness
is a plague to them?

People spit three times for luck,
shield their eyes from the slow
omen of my wings.

If I could fly far higher
than the rain,
in that corridor
of privilege where time defers
to the law of dreams,

such mountains
I could show you then, such nests:
white summits of foam.
I could lay you down gently.

But we go on and on, skimming
the torn black rocks,
finding no sanctuary.

You are heavier than the stones
the village boys once
fed me with.
Cruel your wounds above
the cursed dark field of the sea

le poisson de bonheur

what sea rises in you
what wave stitches you
to the shining void?

again and again I go with you
to the gates
where goodbyes are said

we are in a hospital ward
with lights bright and scathing
as the sun
we are on a Mediterranean shore

there is no oracle here

like a child in the face
of physics
in a condition of ignorance
I thrust the lucky fish
into your hand

the *poisson de bonheur*
rowdy with cheap sequins

it will go with you
inappropriate as the scarf
a mother sends
with her new soldier,
or the honey-cake
baked that morning

if I am not wise
why should I pretend to be?

we are on a white beach, burning –
the Italians are building
an Aztec city in the sand

death has marked you, then,
for extinction
bruised you
with her quick purple shadows

Like someone whose leg has been amputated
but can still feel his toes, so the dead man imagines
the body he has been severed from
by the high surgery of death

my thoughts are sluggish
on the slight tide
and cannot follow
the glimmer of your gay scales,
your leap, Delphic,
at the harbour mouth

to be armless, finned –
is it like the sea breathing,
the way you reach

for nothing, know

no separation
from the great body of radiance?

Votive offerings, Georgiopoli

The salt-white chapel is a ship
of ordinary hopes;

wind battles
at its narrow door, the great
waves cannot gut it.

A deaf ear's stamped in dull tin;
a lone leg, ditto, asks
to walk again;
someone begs for a beaten brass baby.

This year I've learned
that the gods grant
no favours. Today was your
birthday, would have been.

Here's a dumb ikon carved
in amber;
here's a beeswax candle
to light up the stillness, set
fair winds
for your safe passage.

A farewell to Tunisia

We go down gingerly
through pines,
a straggle of dusty tourists
in the limestone throat
of Samaria

From the high blue pinnacles
Zeus picks us out
with his lammergeier's eye

Better if I could believe
it was all his fault,
his hot lightning
that spat at you

The long gorge empties us,
spills us from shade
into the stark open simmer
of the south;
the shore is a parched
mouth the dark sea
bursts on like figs

Black sand silts
the piebald beach,
its bleached crystals,
white and metallic as thought

This is the story
I am coming to know backwards

How can I breathe, swallow,
thinking of houses we won't
inhabit, the choking
bright square of the balcony

and the sea huge beyond, always
the straight blank blameless
edge of the sea

Pieta 3

In the beginning I refused
sympathy, said the only victims
were those torn by war
or murdered
by some truck
on a Turkish highway

Spoke from the bitter guilt
of the survivor

Now I say pity the living who
tremble and are left behind

For I have seen how powerful
the dead are
the way they ignore us
for all eternity

You have gone where nothing
can hurt you, and I
am naked to the thorns

Hard, what you did
hard as your mother's eyes

What ikon on earth addresses me?
Who can I punch and suckle,
what breast

firm as a watermelon
fat with sugar and tears?

like Martha

all along the littoral
the dream-rumour
spreads like wildfire

he is coming back!

already at the station
in the wild uproar
of starlings friends
gather to welcome him

the city opens
like a camellia

the bakers' shops are inundated
with women

like Martha I think only
of the mouths to be fed:

a tide of bread

bread of all denominations
sweet plaited chollas
flat pittas from Izmir
bread full of air and angelica

he has disembarked!

stepped down from the train
with his bicycle
over one shoulder
and a last laugh
for his travelling companions

like Martha I make work
steady the heart

the chairs must be hurried
from the four corners
of the house
the cloth spread square
on the table

generous as a fête
the washing line
shimmies with its bleached sheets

like Martha I am not blessed
and prefer certainty:

does the dream say
that a place must be laid for him?

promise like a prophet
that he will always be
present at the feast?

Moths

all winter the moths
were at their secret feast
in the wardrobe

pale tantalising atoms
they ate sweat
peppered my clothes
with black absence

moths unseen and hungry
moths trembling
in the jaws of time
moths speaking the patient
unacknowledged language
of eternity

even when they flew
into my mouth
like fine ash
I did not hear their warning

all through the dumb frosts
your death fed heedlessly
and hatched in me

by spring, full-fledged,
its whirring wings exploded
from the lace of darkness

field hospital

the tears of my imagination
are legion, like tears bitten back
in the trenches by men in terror
who just get on with it

I can envy sticks and stones,
anything inanimate that doesn't
know it's without you,

or how luck is destroyed,
first suddenly, flaring up
on the wire as if torched
by a phosphorus grenade

and then day by day lies
gangrenous, with its empty eyes
and its dreadful little whisper:
that constant 'oh dear'

think of it:
I am your scalpel
I am your heart cut loose
and panting like a great
blue-eyed dog in summer

what can I drink
that will let the tears flow down?
what can I eat that will make me
forget the gnawing dry hunger
of the dead?

Eros

love, this ghost of bones,
our broken boy,
see how you have charged
me with him

all ruined in the palace
of swallows I call
on you to restore him,
mend him with mud and straw

am I to tell him
that he had a father once
and lost him?

you asked too much
of him, left him
for the cold white lure
of the mountains

I feed him on honey,
clothe his ribs
in the comfort of flesh,
hush and hold him

the sun makes a house
for him, at night the stars
are his peerless nurses

on this island soon
he will suck milk,
tiny as a hummingbird
in his cage of bandages

no one plays in light
like he does, more quietly
than the sea
and all its fishes

when the years bring back
his tongue
he will realise
and I will fear for him

he will rage
at the open road, he will
stand at your rigid door
and shout his desolate questions

Chant

like a stag running to the water
I know my thirst

like a hawk clenched in the high air
I know my hunger

like the fisherman on the river bank
I know the last cold note
when the spirit escapes on a breath

a white frosty page is the land,
this letter we write to one another

in the sky only the geese
come and go with certainty

mind and body I listen, strain
to the four horizons

it's I who am mute, not the invisible
sun shuttered by storms

where is my magic song of the plains
that could bring you back to life
from a bone-shard
like a slain buffalo?

Thalassa

Maybe because I didn't
go looking for you,
when I closed my eyes
we were face to face,

your lost gaze rising
like a star
from the countries
of the sea to burn
once more in the darkness.

Our pillows are mystery-
birds which go
ahead of us. The idea of days
dissolves: the fact is

I can only be alive
here in this safe
place of dreams where
whole multitudes rock
like fish in the cradle
of the waters.

When you crushed me to you
I was inviolable;
I was the sail you rigged,
the hand of the moon
set square on the prow,
the night that wore your name
as death has worn it.

So hard to leave you
when light came, even
if you swore you would come
back again and again
to our sweet bed
to heave gladly
at its oars without thought
of time or the horizon.

The boat, the train

You are waiting on the quay,
the platform
You have been waiting for a long
time

When you gaze at your watch,
bewildered, your dark face
stares back at you
from the harbour

At first the signal
in the distance
is no more than a hum
of air or water,
a fluttering of steel

But then it comes headlong,
by land, by sea it comes,
a precise catalogue
of absence

The crown of a battered
hat in the crowd
The forgotten
outline of a smile

It is the hour of arrival
Speechless, the dogs
of your throat know it

Loss pours over you,
loss tramples you
like a multitude
and fills every seat

So take your place,
it is possible now. Groaning
the train gathers itself,
moves like a glacier
towards the moonlight

The man on the deck

Happiness. Where did it go to?
Yesterday's word muted or forgotten
by the dull blood. When was
it last? Maybe a shiver of sun-

light weeks ago on the winged
shoulder of Staffa, that basalt
angel guarding the mainland
from the westerlies. Or these seals

ringing our wake, their noses
glossy as black cameras. Sweet
puffins battering along
like bees. The bucket of mackerel

picked up in mid-Sound
from the fishing boat,
and the man on the deck
who never raised his head,

just kept sorting furiously,
tearing the crabs and eels
from the snags of the net,
hurling them back to the deeps.

Names of islands Gaelic
and Viking, all echoing
with the facts of the sea
and its authority, what it takes

back and what it teaches:
that some days of your life
will sing to you, and others,
as valid, will break you like an oar.

Bosigran, August 4th

(In Memoriam, Dave Cook)

Bought you a silk shirt
for your birthday, brought
a tea tray up to the bunkroom
with an orange flower on it,
a staunch sea-flower
built for Cornish winds

I can't recall its name, only
that I smashed through wet dead
bracken-stalks to fetch it

On your monkish bed
clenched it in my teeth
till the sun sneaked under my sarong
and found your hands

Later you made breakfast
in the stark kitchen where the men
bickered over guidebooks, your big
bare feet careless of splinters

No, I didn't dream it
It's plain as day, the way
the frying-fat smoked in the sunlight,
the way the climbers barked
with embarrassment, some of them,
the ones set strictly
on manhood, seeing

the silk shirt, the sarong
draped in a slinky skirt
over your sated penis, my happiness
sharp as salt, the ragged flower
heroic in your hair

Reluctance

the kangaroo vine
in the kitchen
thinks it's spring
prinks itself

waves semaphore leaves
at the window

how willingly it waits
for arms of light
to grasp its green
body and rattle its roots

shameless

the weather is mild
as milk
toddlers in the park
trail by, quack
their guileless greetings

time passes
for innocent, a unanimous
parade

daffodil spears
rap out instructions
like cheerleaders:

eyes front!
no more mourning!

Poems 1990–96

The passenger

Earlier I'd been wanting to fly
out of my life. Easy as

sadism to abandon it for some other, probably
in the North, leaving

the meaning of hurt set out
like a delicacy in the empty house

for those who would find it
and eat. I was bitter,

elaborate, in love with the power
of vanishing

In the Underground you can't choose
what touches you. The tall girl, the tumbling

hair that sprang hot
on my shoulder like an animal, breathing

and brushing. I sat still
while it settled, leaned

into it as to a fire
or a welcome

How to explain the need
to harbour, the giving and taking

of comfort; the belly quickened
with sweet dammed-up things –

the whole of my life, its tangling
and untangling

Gossip

On the phone you told me
that the baby weighed heavy
in you: the lost baby, the dead

one, hers, a woman distraught,
a woman not knowing who her child was
or where (the worst)

where he in dread of the dark
had gone (somewhere terrible
she harboured and was sure of,

some chinkless limbo he crouched in
with his sad strange grave-goods
calling and calling for her)

And she, telling you this
so that she might not be mad,

so that your voice, not hers,
would twist like the cord
which throttled him

And now you pass the weight:
the mystery of all he might have said
or loved,

the thousand flowers of language
that waited for him. And later

I too must tell, all of us,
pass him from hand to hand,
make a nest, many,

weave light feathers, help her
to do this; dexterously
unwind the bad shroud,

swear to it: that some
are silenced but everywhere,
and some are nowhere, but

comfortably, and sing
like the wind sings

The Minotaur's complaint

To Ariadne, June's ambivalent, cloud-
stricken, a war between Saturn
and Mars. The sun blares omens,
the earth ripples, volcanic

In the mud of the labyrinth I trample
and sulk. Don't forget
it was Pasiphae who begat me
by a bull-god, guilty
and grunting in that wooden womb.
And now Ariadne's out

to get me, wringing her missionary
hands and slandering: that
white sister, she who crawls
up the virgin sheets, electric,
baring her scent
to the black muzzle of the night

Like mother like daughter.
Afternoons under the tamarisk trees
the shadow-bull battles
in their swooning sleep.
Bent to the mornings's baking
with the sea a blue hum
at the window, they rise
to him like yeast,
scandalous, their faces
turned from each other

Ariadne hoards her prim shame
like honey. When she feasts
on her night fingers, who
is to blame but her brother
the beast, this sticky hybrid
in his sweltering hide

Pay attention to Ariadne. See
how she plots in the nettle-
beds, hears the rumble of hooves
in the maze of her belly:
the quake, the stars
shaken loose

See how she snorts now
at the red entrance
where her horns are, her flared
lips like nostrils, and the nip
of the gold ring that Theseus
might tug and tug

Brêche de Roland

Slow tides of clouds crash, silky, against ridges.
Nothing in me can recall how we came to be
so scant and high. Only you had to go higher,
and rocket back now chalk-faced
with your heart galloping.

You'd been a midge, lonely. I saw you flutter
your arms on the skyline – the signal –
a speck of a thing, helicoptering.
(I'd already taken the photograph)

You'd heard thunder stutter over Spain, scaring
you: nothing but air and vengeance
between you and Africa.

The man from Catalonia cranes politely.
Exhausted, I'm drawing. He doesn't whistle,
breathes some word in the language of humility.

Neither cross-hatching nor cameras
can catch it. When the earth is bare
as a scratched bath and the sky just washes
on through, all you can do is look,

log, rub the brute beasts your feet
have turned to. Finally, retreat inside,
try it from memory. Tell each other,
if God has gates they begin at that blue breach

on the south horizon, that ice-bite
the mouth of the wind sucks at.

Marie Paradis, maidservant

'Ficha moi dans une crevasse et alla ou vo voudra'.

Içi on voit
l'incroyable point
de l'Aiguille . . .

the gentlemen quiver
their staves, wild heads
thrown back, their throats
bared to one another

Mont Blanc like a tablecloth
flung over a banquet,
concealing the *petits cailles*,
hump of the *grosse dinde*,
the geometric gleam
of spoons

In the village they jostle
at telescopes –
six sisters who know, now,
how she wanted to
be somebody: Marie the modest one,
secret as glaciers

In the tottering black
they're laughing and pinching,
taunting her to the edge

Memory. Her face curls back
from the debris of childhood:
Papa smothering
in a crevasse of snowy petticoats

She pants for water,
gathering her weight,
filling her laced boots
with nails. Squatting
like a *grosse dinde*
in her own steam and for what?
Down in the flatlands
she was strong enough
and square, capable
as thumbs

Air streams past her face.
In the cold night the mountain
is a whisper-giant:
her dreams tease her she will
kiss the stars.
La première femme d'Europe,
perched on her father's
high white shoulder.

On the summit her anger arches
like an arrow, sickening
and falling.

Let them spread
their own napkins
on the folds of the snow,
peel the ham from its hot stones.
She will eat pared cheese
hard as a boot:

Ça suffit pour moi,
say the red hands
sullen in her muff.
Champagne at altitude explodes,
she knows it, vanishing
like spindrift
on the blank blue air.

(Marie Paradis, an innkeeper's daughter from Chamonix, was the first woman to ascend Mont Blanc. She was persuaded by her father, who thought that this feat would increase the prosperity of the village by attracting more tourists.)

Haiku, Moniack Mhor

1.

Scottish morning: grey
glue of the porridge-pot
my grandmother left soaking

2.

After years of exile
you forget how the hill sheep
run from the train

3.

Perthshire summer: in the railway
siding, snowploughs
rust among the lupins

4.

Aperitifs on the terrace?
This house
needs a windbreak

Without looking at photographs

Without looking at photographs
there's no one clear memory that would be

incomplete and human, like false hopes,
analysis, or the naked

eye which settles only on the broken
streets between us. What loss

insists on is a whole gold place where
I receive you, where we intersect

with the luminous and forgotten. Nothing
I can say will designate you

or the wild intent
with which I loan myself, listen

like fortune at the far window.
I will play with your face any way

I can, so huge and strange you've become
as you circle the heart of magic.

Song of the Moirai

You will have seen us, momentary
in some dappled doorway, or stark

and bleached
as a white sheet at a crossroads

Unlike Hyacinthus and these other
flower-boys – Adonis, son of Myrrha,

from whose blood anemones
sprang, or Narcissus,

whose grimaces we mimicked
from the mirroring deep

we do not fling ourselves flickering
at death

Rather it is in our nature to be glimpsed
and continue, wordless,

in some shifted shape, to be gripped
and thrown down

Lately we have taken to living
with the fish, these blind friends

of the other senses, who swim
in the parallel ripples of our bellies,

and there we have learnt to weep
three kinds of tears. Some

are like ice, and these are angry
for the hurting world; others

flood the heart and drown out
its light

But the last tears taught to us
are soft as moth-mouths and heal

as they splash on the backs
of our hands. You know

all three of us. Together
we make a line of pure void. Simply

we spin, we apportion,
we are inevitable

Transports

In a locked *Schlaffwagen*, lights and rails
rocking me, I stream south
towards Bavaria

Cities roll through me, the unseen
vineyards. Night words
form and dissolve
like roses torn from the teeth
of the Death Angel

I want to tell you that none of this
is true – these hacked breasts stacked like fish
frosted on the deck
of some Arctic trawler –

that it's only my sleepwalker's mouth
sucking at a cold land angrily.

Rain, rain
on the implacable station
where the white wings of your coat
fly apart. Exile

upon exile. You wish you could set me
free here, dream of drawing me in
and placing me in the light.

Let's eat the bitter herbs, then; dip them
in salt tears. Here is *charoses*, the sweet

spiced apple; horseradish,
fiery as desert sun on the scars of a forgotten
people –

Chosen now,
as I would wish to be chosen, knowing

both the questions and the answers, healed
by the light of a candle, the wine

lifted four times to the lips, the great sea
parting

After Germany

Soon after the smashed border-
posts we come out

of squirrelled woods
and sight Jena. The workers'

flats sail up the hill
like tall ships

tattered by the wide blue sky
of Thuringia

In the alleyways, the old balustrades
drip stucco

(it's policy) and the noses
of angels are gangrenous

The vertigo that was Europe
sucks us on

toward fountains. Let's not stop,
let's keep driving

on the rutted road to Dresden, east,
past the shining

years, past the war
and dumb winter that mothered us.

Crows collapse
into the field. Let's not question

the status of delirium, the hopes
pinned harshly to the breast

of the morning. Somewhere beyond
the broken seas of wheat

Russia will possess us. We have
our boat,

let's not turn back.
In the villages they'll pour milk

into our mouths,
they'll know about drought

and secrets. They'll know
how the heart seeks

lands that are black bread to it,
massed lands, borderless

Persephone's book 1

You say that only when the sun
unstops my mouth and the leaves
pour out like promises
may I send you a letter:
(the speech loosened and green,
or so my dreams have it)

Words wither under the law
In the angry dark my pen
plays tricks on me.
I write:
    to the east, a chilly clear sky
I write:
    the sun low enough to leap over

I do not recognise this rhythm
It is not love but exile
As if taking the word North
and touching it, as if building
with some bright beam
of snow, as if sculpting
where winds are, and essences

I write:
    make virtue of necessity
I write:
    when earth sucks in its children
    what then will go ahead of me
    like a flame on the road?

The truce

Another dawn with black trees
a warlike dawn where negotiations
have broken down
between all parties

Earphones hang from the necks
of exhausted translators

Dawn of silence, but for the
creak of empty escalators

Once words were at home
in this city
mischievous, they rustled
like children's feet on the stairs

They were snapdragons our fingers
rifled in the blue garden

The demagogues have frozen
our words to the walls

Now only the wind moves
in an agony of remembering,

and the flags on the rooftops,
the terrible white flags

Pentecost

In a dark alley of chestnuts the child
beats her heart against a green roof of rain

Blossoms which were tall towers lie
scattered like flaming tongues

Above her head she holds a doll
for shelter from the sky, that basket
which tossed her out like rotten fruit

She wants to say she has been called
to a place other than this, where the gardens
are of dust and pumice-stone

She wants to speak the one molten language
the Syrians understand, and simultaneously
the Elamites, the Cappadocians, the renegade
Jews who stream south through the Gates of Cilicia

She wants to say she is not word alone
but material, sewn from satin and fire,
a red lava of blossoms which pours down
like birdsong on the ever-open ears of the dead

The Forbidden Range, Pembroke

We slant here
here we were left askew
when the land was

Tilted
like the black collapsed
sails of the cliffs
we dip down
into stillness

Windward,
the tide's race,
the blinding green alleys
of the sea:
indifferent, beautiful,
targetted

Here
are the spent shells,
fossil-spines, the iron
sunburst of seaweed

When the gull sheers up
to the grim crown
of the cirque
will we have words
to meet it

Here in pain together,
blessed, water
all around us

Andante

Last night you dreamed
of wrapping the two of us up
in warm turf. Territorial, I told you
this morning as we stumbled
the rain-beaten borders of bean-
fields, where the smell was thick
as lilacs.
A hare's ear tip roared
up the furrows like take-off.
Zip. Later there was some small bitter
death with screaming under the wheat-
stalks, we couldn't see what.
Then hoarse rain, silence,
the wet road cutting between
cornfields. Stereophonic
larks

Pembroke August

In Japan there's a legend
that the first children the gods bore
were a litter of bright islands

Here is another world that floats
on the invisibility of women

I learn etiquette in the shivering
foam: by day, silence, and later
pillow-talk when shadows
soften the rules

In the tent I fall backwards night
after night: the brute sun
of your head sets between my thighs

In the mornings you shake yourself
out like a sleeping-mat;
your monk's eyes retire inwards
to honour the hierarchy of rock-
flakes and buttresses

The beach is a blond garden
of stones, raked immaculately
by the tide

There is a kind of obedience
in the way I follow you
across the brusque turf where metal-
skirted climbers clank like Samurai

My name is strange and seldom
on your tongue. You don't ask,
you can't say, what heat rivets us
to our trouble and paradise

In the meantime it's ridiculous,
the way you eye my inflammatory
breasts and wish we were comrades,

or surge from the sea in your fifty-
year old armour, still thinking
there's a war on

I call on modesty, the oldest
weapon. In the cracked car-
mirror we see the sky we're leaving
is western and on fire,
and later the moon, wicked,
that Japanese courtesan with her black-
toothed smile

Influence

Blossom-blowing time: wind flies
not straight and strident as the crow does
but purposeless, like misplaced snow
when the clouds no longer
practise for winter

Not Rodin's 'errant wind'
which even on still days
agitates the air around cathedrals,
but ludic, unravelling everywhere:
soul upon soul, the white motes
transient as the rose

Not a dance with patterns
and partners, despite the dips
and swoops and soft collisions
of petal against petal;
not even God's huffing
and puffing

Death will come anyway
to blow on your straw house
but now how the sky unfolds
at the four points of the compass,
and how swiftly
something that can't be mapped
takes hold,
senseless and necessary,
a constant sideways shimmying
of the minute skirts of light
and from the no-less-bright air
everything falling

from
Kisses for Mayakovsky

Rannoch Moor

Behind us, Glencoe of the Slaughter,
Achnacone, field of dogs,
Achtriachan, where the water-bull
lurks among thin fish tickled by weed,
and the Great Herdsman of Etive
over us like a black axe

To pace the moor, and mark it,
like a cat bruises the grass
for its bed,
or be claimed instead –
scars of burnt heather, dead
weariness, the sheep paths
misleading, and the bogs
pitted with white water

Slow steps mark the line
on the moor sour with struggle,
where darkness is brought to the brim,
and the bog-cotton bursts
like puffs of smoke
after a musket,
and the broken bleached roots
of the old forest
are white bones under
the petrol shimmer of methane

Slow march in the whine
of telegraph wires,
while the wind chops
at my breath,
and the peat mud sticks to my feet
like rafts

The Great Herdsman of Etive – Buchaille Etive Mor – is a mountain at the east end
of Glencoe.

two women think back

the woman on the TV screen
deliberates   her bedroom
wall blue as midnight
dotted symmetrically
with white stars

she touches her face
her hair   she remembers
her marriage
          exactly
how he peeled her stocking
down
over her ankle

she weeps

the woman in the armchair
watches
         moored
to her short moon shadow
she touches
        her arm
the excellence of her belly

yes it was sweet
that one

she wishes that any marriage
might be remembered so

exactly

by its inconvenient
hurlings
                the willing
legs white idiots
in the air
                the sweet
black scratch of love and lace

Figure in Space, by Giacometti

The art student
in bed with her anatomy books
eats white bread-and-sugar sandwiches.
She pecks white sugar grains
from the pages of bones
and pale plaster scabs
from the moons of her nails

She has forgotten how to speak

She keeps a slush of grey clay
in the kitchen sink
and a postcard pinned
to the wall –
Figure in Space,
with a stride like
open scissors

She will die for Art, starve
for it: they warned her
it might be necessary

They did not say also
that Giacometti was a big man,
muscled, ate like a bear,
enjoyed his lovely wife

On the main street people
loom like hams,
jellied and pink

She will not go out
She will work by the wall
with her stride like scissors

figure
less figure
armature of bird bones
space
more space

Stripping blackcurrants

On a garden rug tinged with amber
your bare skin
grows a red fur.
Half a lilac leaf
sticks to your belly.

Stripping blackcurrants, the berries
split
and stain my fingers
as the stalks
tear from the fruit.

I have a yellow mane which crackles
and brown breasts
freckled as eggs.

Pushing among the leaves, I imagine
their feather fingers
as deft as yours.

Your body haunts the corner
of my eye:
books, papers, your bent head.
I want you in heat,
sticky as blackcurrants.

Deep in the tang of the bush
I remember the taste of your ear.
How you angled your neck
to offer it.

I flaunt my golden back.
It glows from within, a raging aura.
Unbelievable, how you resist me!

You read.
The bush
catches fire.

Significant fevers

A January night. Moonlight
strikes the window. Six sweaters
heaped on the chair,
two pairs of jeans each
containing crumpled knickers.

Proper little girls don't lose their clothes,
the text in the head goes; they fold them
the night before, they dream of piles
of linen neat as new exercise books.

Hot-head, scaly-skinned,
feeble and feverish,
I toss under the weight of quilts.

Liz rings up miserable,
comes round with lemons and whisky.
Her blouse has an ironed crease
down the outside of each sleeve.

Levi-Strauss if I understand him right
says that women disrupt the man-made
opposition between nature and culture.

We nod and drink whisky. The
significance of the fever mounts.

There's no word for the feeling women
have of being in the wrong before
they even open their mouths,
Dale Spender says.

Provisional love. Too much of nothing
can make a woman ill-at-ease.
I'm feeling – *warren*,
hollowburnt. I object to this
set-up, let it be said.

The pale princess on her timid
bed never talks back.
She's dying, but
terribly pleased you asked.

Life is short as a shoelace,
but who knows it?
'68' 1 say, 'the politics of desire –
will we see it again?'
Liz says she wants everything *now*,
everything on offer.
Both of us agree that what we
would most relish at the moment
is to be madly desired. We feel
in the wrong about this too.

Lonelyhearts, Classified:
John, 34, interests: publishing, astrology,
walking. Own car, limited income.
Seeks intelligent feminist 20–40,
Box 288.

I disagree with Liz: No,
they can't all be creeps.
I'm feeling – *oldmould*, *grabbitted*.

In the West, much was made
of killing dragons. St George
and the other heroes with all
their hardware, littering
the ley lines with sites
of slaughter and canonisation.

In the structures of fever,
never a dull moment.
(The spiral round the stone,
the spiral deep in the storm)

In the East they bound
women's feet and believed
in the harmony of man and landscape,
paths of wind, water and dragons,
forces which must not be impeded
by rails, tramways, television aerials.

Sweat stains the sheets. I
have boils, Liz has cold sores:
energies seeking escape routes.

Clean neckties of news announcers,
rescuing us from dragons.
Clean underpants. A consensus.
Under the newsdesk their toes
manipulate electric trainsets.

Proper little girls don't lose their clothes,
the text in the dream goes.
I'm feeling – *ragbitter*,
hellworthy.

The nuclear train which is found
on no timetable sidles
through London in the night,
containing dead hearts blazing:
an energy which has been eaten
and will eat.

Watching the commercials, we note
the speed of the assault, messages
addressed to envy and ego.
We toast each other, high-heeled monsters,
and no country we can name.

'What is good and bad taste is very subjective,'
an ITV executive explains,
of ads shown during a play about women in Auschwitz.
 'Of course we ruled out several categories
immediately – no food or vitamins,
hair preparations, holiday camps,
or gas products of any kind.'
His smile oils the screen.

Clawing at the pillows and the heaped
quilts, *High time*, I say, that the dragon
took hands with the pale princess –
shadow victim defended (sometimes)
by men and lances and smiling
back, always smiling –
first strike in a
quest selfish and long
negative to positive
(I never knew her name)

Take   eat   speak   act

(The spiral deep in the storm,
the world turning over)

Supper

There is the curdling sky
and the green spry beans
finger-long and knuckled
and the bird's flat fleeting path
across my window
and still
you will not come

Border raids

for my grandmother

Fierce pins plough her hair
You can tell by the angry drag
of the net
that once she was beautiful,
envied and glad of it
The nightingale of the county,
electrifying the village halls

She told me she wore winged hats
tall as gladioli,
and the hanging moon sang with her,
and how they clapped and horded
at her doors

When she went,
she went like the old bunch, cursing,
blue as smoke,
you could almost smell the burning
(Oh, they were a wild lot, the Johnstones,
border raiders,
horse stealers setting the Kirk alight
and all their enemies inside)

With her heart tattered
as a tyre on the road
she begged for morphine
and to be done with it,
to be gone among the gliding dead

She glints now in the gooseberry bushes,
her broom hisses out at low-dashing cats
In the night she slaps up her window
and hurls hairbrushes

I've been thinking
If I could go back,
stealing up the cemetery hill
to borrow back her bones,
I'd give her to the merry gods
of the midsummer garden,
who dance among the columbines
who fib and fart
and I'd tell them to trumpet her out

The cliff

The speedwell is blue
in the new bracken,
where midsummer's loose
tumble of daisies
tangles the incline

How good to know
how to shift under the wind,
to be shaken
and rooted

The gull's steep wing
climbs unseen currents,
over the haygatherers
on the headland
and the cattle strayed
in the curling thorn

Three times he will hover
over the prickled cushions
of gorse and the pink
shiver of thrift

Three times he will dive
with his black eye
beating the land flat
and slowing the sea
to a snail's pace

and then he will point south
and slide fast
over the slanting thickets

How good to know
when to go
at the gull's pace,
or grow slow-spiralling
as the hawthorn

to enter the deep
and stinging violet
of the nettle's stem
or drift empty
into the salt air

Friend

In the white morning
we cuddle in our warm
world, toes friendly
in a hoard of blankets,
thighs glossing each other,
bums amiable. Me, I am starved
as a sparrow
after the long cold,
while the snow drives
at tree-trunks,
whirls at my window-sashes,
so fine
it spins
in the cracks and corners
of my house.

Up here
we are in a high galleon
on the crust
of a vanished country.
The sky is iron
behind birds, the road
a track of ash, cracking
with salt, and a scrape and bang
of spades echoes against
the black blocks of streets.

This light
bleaches and blues
skin; our noses of frost
collide.

You are no bully
to dig and spoil, but still
I warn you, some paths
are closed, impassable.

Between my house and yours
lies a city of snowfields;
still I need your steady
heat to set against
the bitterness of winter.

knife

knife my warm handle knife my clasp tight knife my
stroke easy knife my warm cheek my cool blade knife
my flat of the hand knife my slap my safe knife my
finger and thumb no slice i am trim knife my good eye
knife my fly straight knife i am i am my good eye daddy
girl knife my don't cry my see it fly knife my throw my
show it off knife do you like i am my slice my rasp
knife my pink i am i am my dare my red will come knife
my daddy eye good girl knife see it i am i am my blood
my brave my rasp see it my pink pith knife dare do you
like me do you like my gash

In confidence

(for the Writers' Group)

– An orgasm is like an anchovy,
she says,
little, long, and very salty.

– No, it's a caterpillar,
undulating, fat and sweet.

– A sunburst, says the third,
an exploding watermelon:
I had one at Christmas.

– Your body betrays, she says,
one way or another.
Rash and wriggling, it comes
and comes, while your mind
says, Lie low, or go.

– Or else it snarls and shrinks
to the corner of its cage
while your mind, consenting,
whips it on and out,
out in the open and *so* free.

– As for me,
says the last,
if I have them brazen
with birthday candles,
with water faucets
or the handles of Toby Jugs,
I don't care who knows it.
But how few I have –
keep *that* in the dark.

For Maria Burke

(who knocked at the door while I was writing about the alienation of life in the cities under capitalism)

Maria, in search of hospitality:
I opened the door a crack
she stood there in the dark
dribbling a bit.
'We're in need of somewhere to stay.'
She was alone. It was winter.
She wore plimsolls, her bare legs
were hairless.
'I used to know some man who lived here.
It's a squat, isn't it.'
'No, not a squat,' I snapped,
'And who was the man?'

The powerful deeply suspect
the powerless
of manipulations and lying.

'You should come in from the cold.'
Maria's eyes were fixed,
glassy on largactyl.
I phoned some hostels;
she knew them all and
loathed them, said she'd crouch
by frozen trees in the park
rather than go there.
'I went to a house I used to
live in, it was all pulled down.'

Clocks and towers loom over her
Homes shudder and tumble around her.

Her hands shook eating soup.
She accepted tea.
'It's the drug makes me shake.'
She'd hitched from a mental home
in Manchester, heading for another
in Southall, which didn't want her.
'I've a letter from the consultant.
Will you phone for me, tell him
I'm coming in?'

It was dated last June,
it said merely, *Dear Maria,*
it was pleasant to see you
at the hospital today. What
I explained to you is that the drug
is a chemical which acts
on the brain and is necessary
to stabilise the thought processes.

'It's my only home,' said
the orphan angrily. 'I know
they don't want me
but I'm going in. I was there . . .
I lived there . . . three years.'
I showed her the spare room;
she thanked me several times,
stripped to her bra while
I was still there.

Only those with homes are entitled
to modesty; the consultant
is modest, his wife is modest:
her body belongs to him only.
Maria's belongs to anyone:
the mouth to nurses who feed it
the head to doctors who shock it
the nipple to drivers on the open road
who pluck it
the smooth skin to the casual helper.

The consultant, who has all he needs,
considers her promiscuous, recoils
from the glare of the love that
stares from her eyes, seeking.
He reaches for a prescription pad;
this winter, he decides.
Maria must stand
on her own two plimsolls.

Maria gathering up
selves scattered like grit on the road
doodles darkness
and a cottage with lit windows,
gropes and pines for her
three-minute-a-fortnight
father

visit from the antipodes

is it simply because you're coming
that night after night
I dream of being claimed?

as if a switch had been thrown
the pictures flicker back:
that 'fifties marcasite on your black dress
suspender bumps

and I the wolf-child
prowling on packed snow
shimmying stones over the midnight ice

and the snowmen, for delight –
white suitors in the morning yard
with cinder eyes to spin you
round, as debonair as anything

my igloo, too, my hands
never idle, my clever tracery
of sticks and making
on that long ravenous wait to win you

in my factory for happiness
I am mixing you rich as a pudding
I am dressing you like a Christmas tree
you will stretch out your arms and shine

'Il y a longtemps qu'on fait de la politique'

Humming a French song – French-Canadian
that is – remember? I seek out the fireworks.
'Est-ce que vous savez, madame,
ou sont les feux d'artifice?'
– Telling you how I love to be
swept along gay and helpless
behind the baggy-trousered brass band
and the majorettes' fluorescent batons,
how torches and fireflies disarm me.

'It could be Babi Yar,' you growl,
dragging your feet through the fairground,
and the spangled night swings about,
and all innocents are criminals

Il y a longtemps qu'on fait de la politique – Granted;
but need you remind me always
of the dangers of enchantment?
Can't we take holidays occasionally?
Aren't we safe enough here in France
where there's a *kind* of socialism
and uniforms never ever fit
and the majorettes are out of step
and the small boy trombonist
ties up his shoelace in the middle of the encore?

I tell you, we can trust
in these irregular festivities.
See how the village treats us
with *nougat*, with flares and fireworks,
and such sighs sent after soaring rockets,
and how the heads tilt
till they hurt
to see the smoke rush over,
in the stinging sweet
cordite
night

Title from the song by Kate and Anna McGarrigle. Roughly translated – 'We've been doing politics for a long time'.

Pushing forty

Just before winter
we see the trees show
their true colours:
the mad yellow of chestnuts
two maples like blood sisters
the orange beech
braver than lipstick

Pushing forty, we vow
that when the time comes
rather than wither
ladylike and white
we will henna our hair
like Colette, we too
will be gold and red
and go out
in a last wild blaze

August 6th, 1945

In the Enola Gay
five minutes before impact
he whistles a dry tune

Later he will say
that the whole blooming sky
went up like an apricot ice.
Later he will laugh and tremble
at such a surrender, for the eye
of his belly saw Marilyn's skirts
fly over her head for ever

On the river bank
bees drizzle over
hot white rhododendrons

Later she will walk
the dust, a scarlet girl
with her whole stripped skin
at her heel, stuck like an old
shoe sole or mermaid's tail

Later she will lie down
in the flecked black ash
where the people are become
as lizards or salamanders
and, blinded, she will complain:
Mother you are late, so late

Later in dreams he will look
down shrieking and see

        ladybirds
        ladybirds

Heart of April

Upside down
in a magnolia tree
I dangle
in a sea of heaped sky
a soup
brimming with white flowers.

The sky is full of fevers,
greenbronze,
colour of dragons,
and in the city streets
the sour thunder dust
as the air bears low.

Dissatisfaction sounds
like an axe cracking sticks.
I am narrowed down to bones
shin bones across his legs
bones sticking in his teeth.

I will not be a midden-hen,
thin and grubbing,
I am winged and webbed
I am bigger than this
Bright, formless, fluctuating.

Kisses for Mayakovsky

lacy rain
on the window
out there

lazybones
feet up
mooning in the smoke

percolator
spits in the kitchen

the sky
out there
bubbles up with planes

Mayakovsky said
'One must tear happiness
from the days to come'

gasometers bristle
like bad dreams
out there

let us hop like fleas across the lawn

Girls' Gifts

The soft whorls of my fingertips
against snapdragons:
I am making a flower basket for my grandmother.
A rose petal folds back, squares, curls under
One, two, many rose petals curl back
between my fingers
I search for the core which hides.
My grandmother is gentle today,
old. Bees hum over her.
Today she sits reading, not gardening,
not scolding.
The blossom on its branch holds juice which
a touch spills
I glance across the grass,
a shadow in the window is my mother
cooking, watching.
I am making a tiny secret basket for my grandmother.
My mouth waters
I would lick the green leaf, taste the bronze
and yellow silk of my snapdragon,
I mould petals, weave stems, with love
my little finger inches in the folds:
it is done, red and gold.
I will carry it cupped like a jewel or a robin's egg
It will lie, perfect, in her wrinkled palm
I will cross the grass and give it.

from
The Crystal Owl

The Mistresses

Welsh winter: jealous goats
butt to be petted. Long white
cat on my shoulder. Grey dog
with its colonel's eyebrows
hogging the fire. Outside, bantams
to keep from the Christmas fox,
and rabbits aureoled in the torchlight.

You're in the woodshed, mossy-haired
and murdering logs. Your rages
are diurnal, like coast winds
or the rite of milking. Sun-up
and moonrise, these are dead
lovers' limbs in your wheelbarrow.

I appeal to the mirror
and your intelligence. Look
at the silk and size of us,
our fleece and unction.
See how we burn, not wives
but mud witches kneading
the hot udder of the goat,
our laughter glittering
over the white spirt, while
stars pepper our night heads,
and the memories of our loves
festoon us like warm animals.

Alphavillle and after

– 'Savez-vous ce qui transforme la nuit en lumières?'
– 'La poésie.'*
* Lemmy Caution interrogated by computer in Jean-Luc Godard's *Alphaville*.

we never did
    get to Paris
    but yes
    in Usclas
the days opened
like blue shutters
on fictions of other cities

    a bed
    wide as the sea
    the pomegranate
that Persephone-tree,
like a fire in the field

these minutes
    we were married to
    nights
in the underworld
    believing
    we ate people
    possibly
we were gods

just another love poem
    your fruit
    mine
    the light
seeded in our thighs

        unstable bargains
which end like Alphaville:
        Paris snowbound
under a swaying bare light-bulb
        words of love
        reflections of night trains
        nowhere to go

A day like a hotel

In the next room
you light
another cigarette:

blue gauloises
for your earth-
dreams. It's morning,

the wallpaper hour; the house
breathes at your back,
foreign

and pale. Already
you have counted
all you own

as if
you were leaving.
On a day which withholds

pain and pleasure,
your corridors
are polished

to exhaustion,
your blank shoes challenge
in a row

Medusa on Skyros

in the parading square
  where glossed nations
    muddle
      in their young
    Eurotans
  a woman
whose bruised face
  bags
    and bounces
      when she laughs
    raises
  her bright brown
wig
  to the men
    of middling age
    who have been flirting
cool and kingly
  into her eyes
    into the deep stretched silk
      of her breasts
    and oh
  they go
ghostly –
  ai! ai!
    in the rattle
    of all the small
    ouzo bottles
  as she flaunts
their sudden skulls
  grinning
    in the bristle
      of her short grey hair

The skating lesson

After all this time he is going home
with his hope like a hammer
and his unfinished eyes,
but first he is teaching you
frost and balance.

(No need to lie, under
the red skirt of summer
we were liquid and mad,
orchards to each other –
how will he explain this away?)

Cold-nosed he is dancing backwards,
holding out his arms.
(His scissor-spin and snap,
his Hey Lady grin
and his heart bolting)

Make no mistakes
Don't tax him
Listen to the organ's
chronic electric song.
The light on the ice is wet.
Don't look into it. Think dry.
Below you the blades grey
as fish teeth and harsh.
Push right. Push left.
You love. You move, you move.

Cornfield with skylark

On 30th March 1987, Van Gogh's 'Sunflowers' was sold at Sotheby's for 25 million pounds.

Close up. Coins
stirred in the wet
of a café table

luminously, a blotched
letter:
My dear generous Theo

Long shot. The North
Sea shouldering
at sluice-gates:

Holland, where windows
measure wealth
and the sun

is thin as scorn. Perhaps
it is as his father
said

all he accumulates
is lack

(the black eyes
of the cornflower
stars, roar

of the sun in his head,
the sinless sky
circling the bright

wheat,
the church tower tortured
or rejoicing)

Close up. Coins,
a letter:
this one for blood –

money, this
for the magpies

with their stolen
bitter news

(fallen
cherry-blossom, the gutters
are steep screes of it)

Liberating Dachau

Impossible to even think of,
the cameraman says, with that

bald freeze of dolls at the back
of his eyes. He says they had been

gnawing at themselves, and possibly
at each other. He says the snow

shrouded them, stroked them like fox-
fur, their caved chests, their hopeless

pajamas. (Poles, Byelorussians, the odd
Communist. One was a bad barber, one

a mender of clocks, one broke women
like bright leaves)

They hang now, they are braced
and shrunk, the dimensions

drawn out of them. (The trance,
the tale, the white stir of water,

the wheel of sparks.) Impossible
to even think of such robbery.

The blanched dead are boxed
in the mirrors of their eyes

Their hair fritters to light
nets in the mackerel sky

Their hair falls from the still
firs to enter our mouths

Freeze-frame

1947. That winter they talk of.
A winter like fists or wizards,

one or the other. The frozen lawn
pitted with porridge and scraps,

soup-bone fat with marrow
that the crows brawl over,

big sister buttoned up
with her puppet gloves dangling.

For background, there's the gable
where old Jessie lived,

a black wedge, and her
the witch of a hundred cats,

reading
your mind's eye, your bad eye.

1947. Small birds dumb as dolls
on the winter wire. I saw

their hearts like peas
and pitied them

that they were never born with tongues
to tell us things. I emptied

my wishes up chimneys, insisted
on reindeer.

Click of the camera fixes
my mittened hand to a blur:

the snowball's invisible as anger
shuttered in the nick of time.

My sister is too patient,
with her face like Petrouchka

and her snow-drifted smile.
She has no tongue, she says

nothing, thinks of Jessie
with the soot under her skirts

and the cats
wicked on the wall.

Sorority

we are here
we work quietly
in empty rooms

we stroke
the spokes of the poem

it is the dream
it is the new blue dress
we want to keep secret
yet wear in the open

it is the guest
at the threshold
the host
waiting stretched
and delicate as a parasol

from light
or from darkness
someone who loves us
is coming
hurrying
over the hungry world

Pigeons

Pigeons
are tossing up
seeds
and bread.
Their pecking is snappish,
they want
what they want
and the rest
goes in whirligigs
like salt over their shoulders.

Today
when I said
I was writing about you –
for women will make meat and bread
of their long tearings –
you looked like that puffed
angry one
in its purple ruff;

yes,
that's
what you looked like.

Cassandra flies Olympic

five miles high above Athens
something ancient
tells her she's in for it

this little fleeing ton of metal
fat as a brick
can clatter down the unsafe sky

some debris of birds or gods
ripping the jets apart, or else
the tailplane nipped off
by satellite peelings

if she could only cry oracular
along the blond coffin of faces
which talk rockabye
and beer
and living rooms

we will fall off the edge
of a wall of wind
we will tumble back down
to the tossed thick sea
and the blue ships

can't they see the collision
in her face, already
like a robbed nest, chaotic
with glue and shell-shards and feathers?

when the music changes

the dutch girl settles
her black cigarette-lighter
exactly on the edge of the music

her sitting is a statement
which flowers
only in these chords, this
café table, the scoured dry blue
backdrop of mountains,

an emptiness into which
some something must,
she thinks,
come spiralling

won't you please
the waiting, the glamour
of the guitar crying out,
won't you please read my sign,
be a gypsy

the music does it, the magic
is all made for her:
the glass lie, the slipper
that fits
tell me what I want to find.
deep within me

when the music changes, a frown
will sting her face, for now
nothing speaks for her, only
her bare shoulders,
her black cigarette-lighter,
the thin thumb
lightly pecking her mouth

the words to say it

in the night the words come down
dream peacocks strutting for dear life
in the noise of the field and the birds in it

trailing for mates, blue winds fan
their great tails
(their tails spreading dust and rainbows,
their insolent rant of happiness)

this is how, loving and speaking, we
quake, moon, embrace, until dawn
aches across the bed, ghosts
and colours are dumb
and morning makes me a
house of nonsense
stains of teabags
flat shadows burned into the walls
the telephone city tinkling to itself –

light, garrulous, how *are* you?

heart-breaker

wheelchair lady
approaching 100 years old
in white straw hat
with pink petunia
and fine angry eyes on me
because she too
was once long as a lily
and in love
because today
they tucked her disastrous limbs
neatly sideways
and dressed her for holidays
and she thinks I don't know
petunia was her colour
the one she stung
and blistered in
and she thinks I don't know
what laughter seamed
her quartz and cunning face
and she thinks I don't know
what's coming to me

Scapegoat

(the reunion, New Zealand)

in the house on the ridge
above the valley of apples
where Dutchmen shake out their golden hair

we are the daughters of delight
welcomed in our silver and better selves

we eat
sweet tea/wool/rings grinding as glass
our scones in the oven are chubby as cupids

mother pours earrings on us
her teeth are bracelets on the night table

sun moons across the north
moon wanes backwards

here in the antarctic
where nothing is accurate
she/they/we are pierced by sleep

mother shoos a rooster:
foul-footed you are,
always pestering the poor chooks

her red face scolding wildly
her wild red face trying to be none the wiser

ungrateful bird she has filled and fed
bird full of apples and worms

sister says he is greedy and not good
selfish like all men and we have held
our tempers too long

shit-spray of fear on the carpet
upside down it seems as tall as she
the heavy bird shaken like a wet lettuce

our red faces laughing wildly
at its gaping affronted beak
our wild red faces trying to be none the wiser

am I good not greedy
am I important as anyone
am I honey in the crack of the rock

The Rothko room

Scarlet let the sun in
under my thumb, but now winter

is truer, maroon has a weight
the air gasps in and out of

I have stopped straining
in bare space

to hear echoes of engines
push the frost to slush

Beyond the window
summer is a blare

At the intersection the dizzy
whites of their clothes

whisk my eyes like eggs
this way and that way

Up out of the subway
people are carrying suitcases

Four black horses rear
against the evening

In the queer sack of illness
I am knifed and safe

So little movement now
except in skies and those

who skid and are bright
on the scarlet crust of the city

Postscriptcard

This is where we were
when the moon
nipped at us.
I've marked the bed-
room with a cross.
Believe me,
we were cheap, we were
in heaven, we were
forgetting how to lie.
Wish I was here. Love
me

Naturally

I expect you'll see her
one day soon
in dappled rain,
naturally,
at the park gates
or by the canal

Probably you'll carry
a tennis racquet,
and when something says
She's back
you'll ask yourself
who speaks
and marvellously stop seeing
traffic lights and irises

because you'll be watching yourself
wondering
is this me
my steady hand
my slow blue veins
my elaborate arm hanging
naturally

I expect she'll brush past
without touching
your mouth
and you'll ask yourself
is this me
my bucket of bees
my strung bones
frantic with laughter

but you'll be watching yourself
wondering
if the chalk on your tongue
is the sadness
you didn't suck from her

Rodin's muse

She writhes like hawthorns,
is dark and demented,
her impossibly heavy head
a branch of thoughts the winds
have knotted. In all violence

she loans herself (this muse
who promised him a flat blue slate
to shine his shadow on)
Her calves are rivers
from the glacial snout,

her bruised elbows abut
a space mute and compressing
as rock. The torture starts
not in the lovely torque
of the belly, or even
gravity itself

(this muse who gives no release,
is not delicate, does not dance)
but in a black burning at the pit
of the throat, a capture
of pain and angles somewhere
between his heart and her silence.

'A tender youth without fault or blemish'

'And this was what Findabhair used to say afterwards of any beautiful thing which she saw, that she thought it more beautiful to see Froech across the dark pool; the body so white and the hair so lovely, the face so shapely, the eye so blue, and he a tender youth without fault or blemish, with face narrow below and broad above, and he straight and spotless, and the branch with the red berries between the throat and the white face . . .'

Irish, eighth century, author unknown

The wings of the mountain
spread out around us
The leagues of the night
move in us, and the moon
with its pale firs,
its black aching rowanberries

The moths
couple like kisses
The woods fall back
to welcome us

In the high ice we burn ourselves
on air and wine

The mouths of mystery exist
and have spoken for us:

A desire unto death.
We draw near and far,
weak-limbed, gigantic

O welcome the flame of the rowan
O welcome our small steps, our long leagues
O welcome the drunk moon and its tongue of tribes

Fantasia for Mary Wollstonecraft

There's the same view:
mottled streets, the squat
chapel, the boys
on the spring streets
still raucous
and glossed as blackbirds,

yodelling out
for just anybody
and oh
breakneck Mary
how we go round
on the great wheel of April,
to be tugged or broken,
pushed out
still streaked and yolked,
our skin
transparent to the blood

You're here, old bully
at my right ear,
storming radically up
to a broken blue place
where girls will grow
unimaginably into themselves

Your pen leaps across
this blown and blinding day
in the city,
and the dream is
to dare everything – horses,
defeats, vendettas –
to act with a raw edge

Or else you go hungry,
and your thoughts
are the colour of spiders –
that tittering in the distance,
this drab woman
with her schoolmistressy smile,
does she presume?

He's with that actress again,
that pepper-and-salt
rouge-pot, everybody
knows it;
but you don't pine
when your mind is a knife
to slice with –

Into the river, then,
on an oily night without stars,
under the spars of the bridge
your stupid hem
bloating up. Blundering yards
of petticoats floating you,
and even your dense energy
won't take you down.

Indestructible Mary,
how you sigh
on your dry beach,
the days
sit in your mouth like stones.
Saying you stay alive
only for superior tasks –
all your frippery sisters
just asking to be put in order,
and ardent France, too,
tearing at you like a red
trumpet.

You want fresh strength,
possibilities of men
and mercy and to give
and give, to see love
and revel in the rights
and wrongs of it,
to look it in the teeth. No masks,
now or ever.

Timid Godwin
trembles at your relish –
all this
under the woman's skirts,
desire
silver down her spine,
and doesn't she dance
on his wounds,
teasing and smirking?

The quarrels raking you together,
a stubborn gathering
of two donkeys thinking freely
and biting each other –
so who the devil
would think he'd turn husbandly
and you hold still
and temper
for the child's sake?

Mooning Mary
on a winning streak,
this next birth
will be different.

September-smoky
and encircled by love,
it will be fierce fruit,
a gay
deliverance.
It will give you Godwin,
too, irreversibly,
(this day with the name
of your real death)

Modern Mary
you have travelled
and arrived, yet in the heat
of the heart of it,
a terrible fever
pins you to yourself.
Such ravishing cold –
Nothing
was ever meant to be like this.

Blackbirds' wings
like a sudden fast scratching
and even as you
shake your life out
they are using you
singularly
to stifle their girls –

Oh shocking
Mary, you strumpet   you
plural woman   you
plainest prophet

Below the *Ecrins*

You can be neck-high wet
    in the woods here
where raspberries drip and shine
    Or still
in the shouting field
    where crickets nubbled
and grey as graves
    tick hot time away

Or again, huddled
    in the white window's riot
when the *patron* stops dead, high lightning
    tilting his face like a ship

In the valley there are no strangers
    Down here
there's the tender twist
    and fuss of flesh,
the luxury of gasps. We shiver,
    knowing what we know
In the radio burr,
    only the eyes show it

Up there we would be mere pepper
    tossed on the storm
Up there the mountains are pared bare
    by the arbitrary disciplines of heaven

And the clouds are the white flowers
    of the moon
And the seracs are the white teeth
    of the moon

Light bulbs ping
        in the purpling dark. Even
the hands of the card-players
        lose their cunning

Up there you skim clear as a razor
        over your hollowing heart
Your strange heart
        in this blue egg of silence
on the morning you have never been to before

Rune

Sweet knot of space that the body briefly is
Mouths that all air and kisses enter
The snowstorm, radiant in passing
Wild darkness of all light-filled things